A French song

This is a song from France. It is written in an unusual way.

Because the melody starts halfway through the first bar, the first strong beat is not on the first note of the phrase.

The style of a folk song so is a clue to country it comes from.

All the girls of La Rochelle Built a ship to sail the sea, Built a ship to sail the sea. And to travel o'er the ocean To the land of Italy. Oh, the wind, the wind's a-scatt'ring All the leaves from off the tree.

Sing the song, tapping the pulse.

As you sing, tap the strong first beat of the bar with your fingertips, and all the other beats with the back of your fingers.

Work with a partner, if you wish.

The half-bar entry (1) p.77

A melody jigsaw

You have learned the song 'J'ai du bon tabac' with your teacher.
It is a French melody which starts at the half bar.

Here is the beginning and end of each line:

Each piece of the jigsaw is a bar of the melody.
But they are not in the right order for 'J'ai du bon tabac'.

With a partner, work out the order of the bars.
Write down the number order of the jigsaw pieces.

2   The half-bar entry (2)   p.77

Farandole

This is a French dance, called a Farandole. It is a lively dance, usually in 6/8 time. This Farandole uses a lah pentachord.

The Farandole is usually accompanied by a tambourin (a small drum).

Sing the melody to solfa, then play it on a keyboard or xylophone.
(There may be members of your class who could play it on a recorder, or some other wind instrument.)

lah

Find a partner to play this rhythm on a small drum as an accompaniment to your piece.

Your teacher will explain how to dance the Farandole.

Music for the dance p.78

Semitones

Sing this hexachord with a partner.
Listen for the semitones.

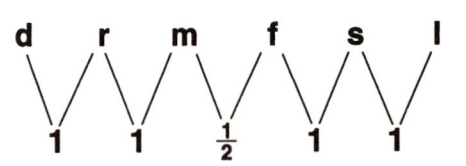

Play this hexachord on a keyboard instrument.
Look for the semitones.

Sing this hexachord with a partner.
Listen for the semitones.

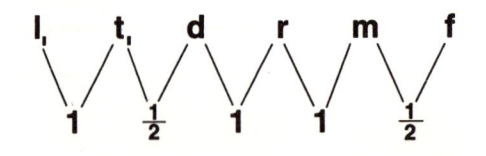

Play this hexachord on a keyboard instrument.
Look for the semitones.

Work with a partner.
By singing and playing (lah = A), improvise lah hexachord melodies.
Enjoy having two semitones to use.

4 The hexachord on lah (1). The semitone   p.79

Working with semitones

Sing this melody to solfa, with a partner.

Then sing it in turns to each other until you can both sing it from memory.

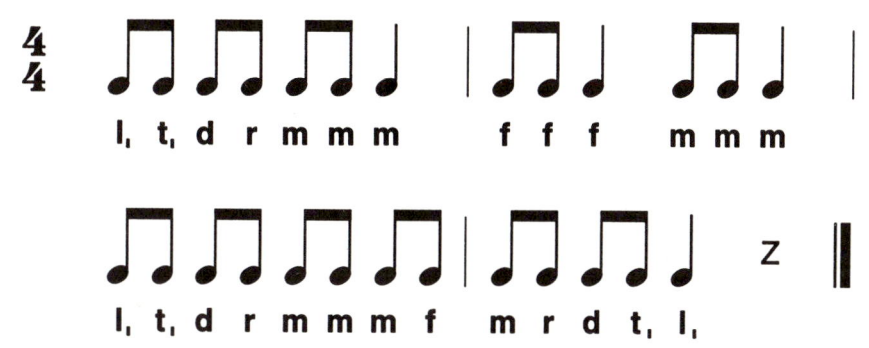

$\frac{4}{4}$

l, t, d r m m m   f f f   m m m

l, t, d r m m m f   m r d t, l,

Using your memories only and without reading, play the melody together on xylophones or on keyboards (lah = A).

Notice where the semitones occur in this melody.
How many semitones are there?

Play up and down the keyboard in semitones, using all black and white notes in turn, as they occur.
Notice that there is no black note between B and C.
Notice that there is no black note between E and F.
So, B – C and E – F are also semitones.

The hexachord on lah (2)   p.79

Using your musical ear

Here is the lah hexachord on D:

Work with a partner.
Play from memory the page 5 melody on a keyboard, this time starting on D.

Talk with your partner about it – and then look at this:

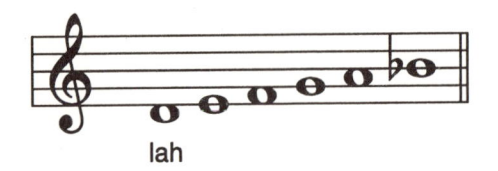

Your ear tells you that a B flat is needed.
This places the semitone correctly.

Play the melody on page 5 again, but this time with lah = G.

What does your ear tell you about the flats needed for the lah hexachord on G?

Write these hexachords on Writing Sheet 1.
Write in the 'flat' signs where they occur.

Using the lah hexachord   p.79   1

Hanukkah

Sing this melody to solfa with a partner.
Learn to sing it from memory.
Play the melody on a keyboard.
Notice the way the B flat is shown.

One for each night, they__ shed a sweet light. To re - mind us of days long a - go.

One for each night, they__ shed a sweet light. To re - mind us of days long a - go.

The melody can also be written like this, using fewer bars:

One for each night, they__ shed a sweet light. To re - mind us of days long a - go.   - mind us of days long a - go.

After the first time bar, go back to the beginning –
jumping to the second time bar on the repeat.

The lah hexachord on D. The flat   p.81

A Flemish melody

The upper part of this piece is a Flemish melody (doh hexachord on F).

Lyrics (upper part): A lit-tle child on the earth has been born. He came to the earth for the sake of us all. sake of us all.

Lyrics (lower part): A lit-tle child came to earth for us all for us all.

Notice the B flats. Only one flat is needed in each bar.

Sing this with a partner in two parts, using solfa. Make all the repeats shown.

When you can sing it in parts, play it on two instruments –
two recorders, two keyboards or two glockenspiels.
Then perform it on two different instruments – for example, recorder and glockenspiel.

8   The doh hexachord on F   p.82

'Temple Barr'

Here is an English country dance melody, called 'Temple Barr'.
Play it on your keyboard or pitched percussion instrument.

lah

Fine

D.C. al Fine

What is the tone-set for the first section?
What is the tone-set for the second section?

Improvising

1. Partner 1 plays the first section.

2. Without pause or change of tempo, partner 2 improvises a new four bars for the second section (doh hexachord on F).

3. The first partner repeats the first section.

4. Now change roles, with partner 2 playing the first section and partner 1 doing the improvising.

The tonalities of doh and lah hexachords   p.83

Strong rhythm

This Slovakian folk melody has a distinct East European style.
As it has a strong rhythm, it is suitable for dancing as well as singing.

lah

One partner sings, while the other taps this ostinato rhythm:

One partner plays on a keyboard, while the other taps this ostinato rhythm on a percussion instrument.

Sing it, while tapping the rhythm yourself.

Recognising tonality   p.84

A Slovakian dance

The phrases of the melody on page 10 are either lah-based or doh-based. Each phrase has its own tonality. Hum the melody, decide on the tonalities, and see if you agree with the table below.

PHRASE	TONALITY
1	lah
2	doh
3	lah
4	lah

This may be played as a second part to the melody on page 10:

Compose a dance in 6/8 time, with a similar structure.
Change tonality where you feel it to be most suitable.
Write your dance in staff notation (lah = D).

Working with tonalities p.84

Working with fanfares

Here is a march for a very important ceremony:

soh

Here are two fanfares to play with the march:

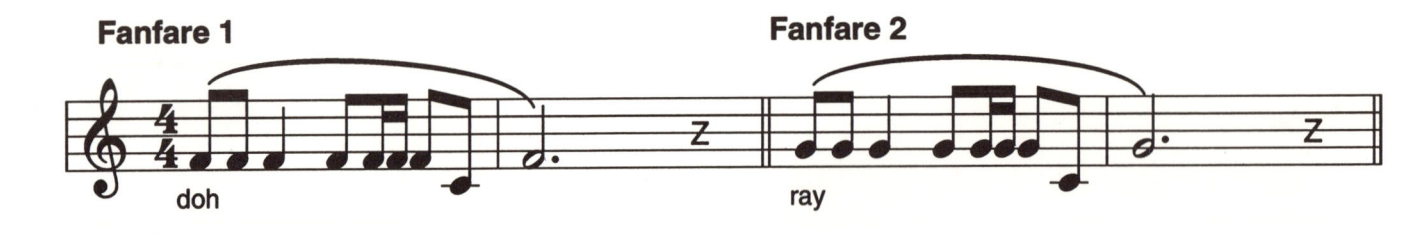

Fanfare 1

doh

Fanfare 2

ray

With a partner, play the march until you are confident. Then play the two fanfares.

Play the march again, with one partner playing Fanfare 1.

If Fanfare 1 is played all the time
it is monotonous and not always pleasing;
so, in which phrase of the march would you use Fanfare 2?

MUSIC IN OUR LIVES

For the occasion: ceremonial march (1)   p.85

March for a grand occasion

The organiser of the ceremonial occasion has asked that the march (on page 12) be longer to give more time for the procession to reach the end of the parade ground.

So, compose 8 bars more (called section B).
Change the tonality throughout this section to lah = D.
Write your section B in staff notation.
Add fanfares if you wish.

MUSIC IN OUR LIVES

Make a recording of a performance of your march.

Then perform the longer march – with the structure A B A.

A percussion accompaniment (e.g. drums, cymbals) is necessary for a march.

Remember that marches are often played in large, open spaces.
So perform your march with instruments which can be taken outside.

Perhaps the class could use the playground for a march past, accompanied by the class band.

For the occasion: ceremonial march (2) p.85

Ally bally

Robert Coltart made his own sweets and candies. He used to sell them in the streets and markets of the Scottish border towns.
They must have been very good sweets because the children would pester their mothers for pennies when they knew that Robert was coming to their town.

'Ally bally' is a Scottish folk song.

Al - ly bal - ly al - ly bal - ly bee, Sit - tin' on your Mam - my's knee,

(Greetin' means 'crying'; bawbee means 'penny')

Greet - in' for an - ith - er baw - bee tae buy mair Coul - ter's can - dy.

Sing the song to solfa with a partner.
Think about the words. What tempo is most suitable?

This song uses a doh hexachord.
Because doh = F, a B flat has been placed at the beginning of the staff.
This is called a **key signature**.
The key signature makes it unnecessary to write a B flat every time it occurs in the melody.

14 The key signature (1)   p.86

Changing tonalities

The melody on page 14 has three phrases.
All three phrases are of doh tonality.

phrase 1	phrase 2	phrase 3
doh	doh	doh

Form a group of three people.
Together, sing 'Ally bally' again – using solfa names.
The song uses the doh hexachord on F and starts on doh.
Then sing the song again, with each member of the group singing a phrase in turn – using solfa names.

Now, sing the melody as if it used the lah hexachord on D and started on lah.
Notice the change of tonality.
In your group of three, sing a phrase each in turn, remembering to start on lah.

phrase 1	phrase 2	phrase 3
lah	lah	lah

So the new version begins:

l, d m m   f f f f   m   etc.

Now sing the melody as if the phrases changed tonality. For example:

phrase 1	phrase 2	phrase 3
doh	lah	doh

How many versions can you make?
Which do you prefer?

The key signature (2)   p.86

'I saw . . .'

With a partner, sing from memory 'I saw three ships'.

It is a doh hexachordal melody.
Sing it to solfa.

Then, from memory, play it on a keyboard (doh = G).

This melody can be played in another position on the keyboard, without black notes, with doh = ? .

Sing this piece.
It is a second part for 'I saw three ships'.
Sing it as your partner sings the melody.
Listen for the semitones.

Working with the doh hexachord on F (1)   p.87

...three ships'

Write 'I saw three ships' in staff notation, with doh = F and a B flat at the beginning of the staff.

Sing your melody to solfa, and add the words.

With a partner, perform 'I saw three ships' in two parts on instruments, playing the melody from memory and reading the second part from page 16.

'I saw three ships' is written in $\frac{6}{8}$ time – a compound time signature.

With a partner, and singing to solfa, think how you might adjust the melody so that it becomes a simple time melody in $\frac{4}{4}$.

Some delayed notes would add interest.

So your version might begin: $\frac{4}{4}$ ♩ | ♩ ♩ ♩. ♪ | ♩ ♩ ♩ etc.

                                                                                      d   d d d   l   s f m

Can you make the melody sound as successful in simple time as it does in compound time?

Working with the doh hexachord on F (2)   p.87

At the disco

Here is a song in the style of pop music. With a partner, sing the song slowly to solfa and then play it on an instrument.

MUSIC IN OUR LIVES

soh

Come rain or shine, or a - ny wea - ther, It's al - ways fine when we're to - ge - ther, Come rain or shine, or a - ny wea - ther, You are the one for me, You are the one.

1. What - e - ver
2. *Fine* hap - pens we shall al - ways be the best of friends, you'll see;

D.C. al Fine

At times of dark - ness and ad - ver - si - ty we'll make sweet har - mo - ny.

At the disco (1) p.88

Disco dancing

When you are confident, perform the song in the right style, with one partner playing on a drum, or tambour.

Play *either* 4 strong beats per bar,
      or with alternate strong beats.

Try accompanying the song with a pre-set pop or disco drum rhythm from your keyboard.

Notice how the melody repeats.

Ask your teacher if the class could dance to the melody and rhythm accompaniment.

Look carefully in the song on page 18 to find any of the following features:

- tied notes
- repetition
- sequence
- upper/lower parts of the tone-set
- key signature
- half-bar entry.

MUSIC IN OUR LIVES

At the disco (2) p.88

19

Fly, little nightingale

In ancient Greek, the word 'poly' means 'many' and 'phony' means 'sound'. Music which is composed of strands of melody, like the piece on this page, is called **polyphony**.

Sing the piece with a partner.

Josquin des Près wrote his music 500 years ago. He spent most of his long life as a musician in Italy, but he was born in the country we now call Belgium. His music was religious music, for performing in church, and sung in Latin. The English words have been added recently.

Prepare Writing Sheet 1 for staff notation in two parts.
Write out the piece, with doh = C.
The tone-set is the doh hexachord + t_l.
Invent new words for a second verse for this version.

Working with canons (1) p.90 1

A Mozart canon

Josquin's music on page 20 is a canon.
Here is another canon – by Mozart, who was born in Austria.

Mozart's canon is different from Josquin's in several ways.
Can you find some of the differences?

Notice that one part is changed slightly at the end so
that both parts finish together.

Sing this Mozart canon with a partner.
Then perform it by humming.
Then play the canon on two suitable instruments.

Working with canons (2) p.90

A Zulu song

This is a Zulu song from South Africa.
It uses the doh hexachord on D
– so every note F becomes an F sharp (♯).
You can see the F♯ at the beginning of each staff.

Way, way - oh - way, Oh the li - on,
One and one and one and one, and put a peb - ble here.

Your teacher will explain the stone-passing game.

When you can play the game well, invent a rhythm to play on a drum as the melody is sung.

1 Work to a steady pulse.
2 Make your rhythm contrast with the rhythm of the melody.

Choose the best rhythm in the class, and perform it with the song as the game is played.

22   The doh hexachord on D (1)   p.91

Games galore

Choose one of these activites, using the doh hexachord on D:

1. Compose your own stick- or stone-passing game.
   Use suitable words and write your melody in staff notation. Try to use delayed notes and/or sequence in your song.

2. Invent a game of your own, and write the words and melody for it.
   Perhaps it could be a circle game, an action song for small children, a ball game or a skipping game.

Compare the results with others by playing the games in class or in the playground. Decide which game is enjoyed most and teach it to other children.

The doh hexachord on D (2)   p.92

Beachcombers

Beachcombers

1. *Searching in the driftwood,*
   What shall we find?
   Seaweed and bottletops –
   Old bacon rind.

2. *Searching in the flotsam,*
   What shall we see?
   Chemicals and plastic bags –
   Someone's picnic tea.

3. *Searching in the jetsam,*
   What shall we spy?
   Old bones and bicycles –
   Birds that used to fly.

4. *Searching for a clean world,*
   What can we do?
   Care of the environment
   Begins with me and you!

Say the words of the first verse to a metre of $\frac{4}{4}$ or $\frac{2}{4}$.
Write the rhythm of the words.

Say them again, but this time in $\frac{6}{8}$.
Write down your rhythm.

Say them again, but this time in $\frac{3}{4}$.
Write down your rhythm.

It is worth remembering that syllables can be sung to more than one note.

- Choose the rhythm you like best as a basis for composing a melody for these words.
- Use the doh hexachord on D.
- Decide on the structure of your melody.
- Write your melody in staff notation.
- Make sure that the melody can also be used for verses 2, 3 and 4.
- Sing your song to a partner. Can your partner suggest improvements?

Composing: doh hexachord on D p.93 1

Shepherd's hey

This is a famous English folk dance melody.

Sing, then play the melody. Learn to play the melody from memory.

If you have enough instruments, play the melody from memory as a whole class.

From memory, play the melody with doh = G, and doh = F.

Shepherd's hey p.93

A Serbian melody

This melody is based on the lah hexachord on E.
Notice the F♯ key signature.

On the o - pen road I go, Stars at night to guide me. If the storms and winds do blow

Then my tent will hide me. I hear mu - sic soft and slow

In the val - ley deep be - low; Shep - herd,

play your sweet re - frain, Bring us peace of mind a - gain.

Sing the melody with a partner.
Work out, and write down, the rhythm-set for this melody.
Using elements from its rhythm-set, invent
an ostinato rhythm to perform with this song.
One partner performs the melody,
as the other performs the rhythm ostinato.
Then, taking turns on your own, perform the melody and
the ostinato at the same time.

26   lah hexachord on E   p.94

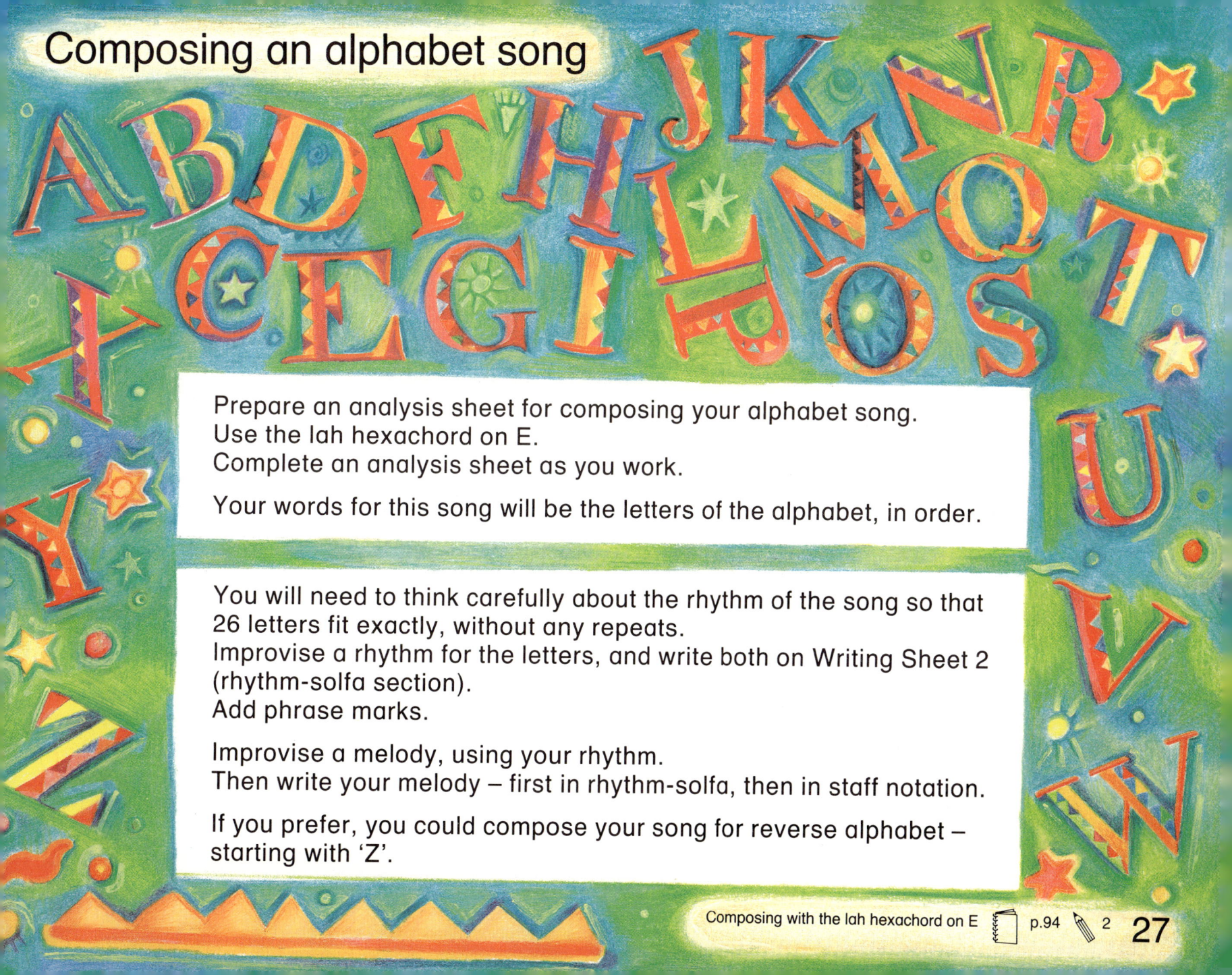

Composing an alphabet song

Prepare an analysis sheet for composing your alphabet song.
Use the lah hexachord on E.
Complete an analysis sheet as you work.

Your words for this song will be the letters of the alphabet, in order.

You will need to think carefully about the rhythm of the song so that 26 letters fit exactly, without any repeats.
Improvise a rhythm for the letters, and write both on Writing Sheet 2 (rhythm-solfa section).
Add phrase marks.

Improvise a melody, using your rhythm.
Then write your melody – first in rhythm-solfa, then in staff notation.

If you prefer, you could compose your song for reverse alphabet – starting with 'Z'.

Composing with the lah hexachord on E   p.94   2

Architecture in music

The designing of a bridge needs to be done skilfully if the bridge is not to fall down.

The designing of a longer bridge needs even more careful thought. For a long bridge to be safe, the designer will often plan in sections.

In a similar way, longer melodies are designed and constructed in sections.

Use this plan to compose a longer melody, or draw up your plan using similar ideas.
Compose in staff notation.

SECTION 1	SECTION 2	SECTION 3
2/4 doh hexachord on F	lah hexachord on D	doh hexachord on F
8 bars / 2 phrases (A Av)	8 bars / 2 phrases (B Bv)	8 bars / 2 phrases (A Av)
Include: delayed notes	Include: sequence	Include: delayed notes
Include: ♫ ♬		Include: ♫ ♬

Compose a melody for instruments, suitable for dancing.

Structure: changing tonalities p.95

Syncopation

You may have sung this melody before. Sing it with a partner, while tapping a steady pulse of 4 beats to each bar.

A-lice the ca-mel has five humps, A-lice the ca-mel has five humps, A-lice the ca-mel has five humps, so go, A-lice, go.

Notice how certain stresses in the rhythm occur between the beats. For example:

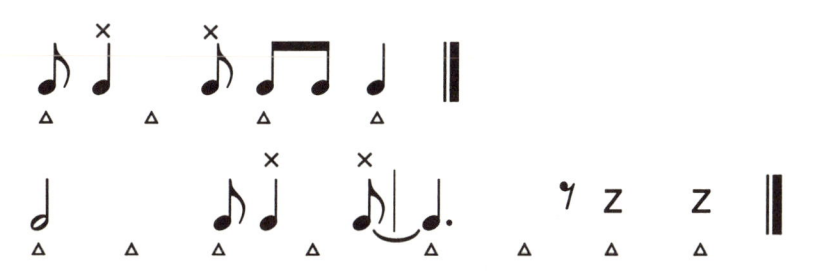

These are called *syncopated rhythms*. They can have musical meaning only if you keep to a steady tempo.

Syncopation can add great excitement to music.

Choose one of these rhythms and perform it as an ostinato, as your partner sings or plays the melody.

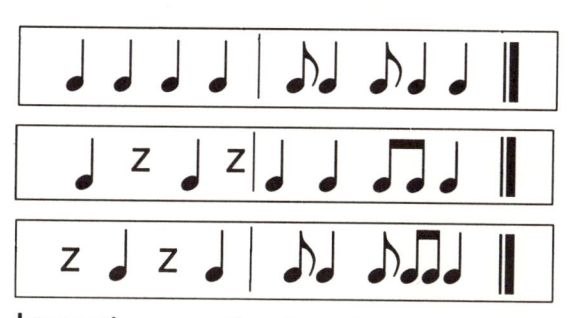

Invent an ostinato of your own (adding a touch of syncopation).

An Irish melody

And now, my lads be of good cheer, for the I-rish land will soon draw near, In a few days more we'll sight Cape Clear, O Jen-ny get your oat-cakes done. Whip jam-bo-ree, whip jam-bo-ree, O you pig-tailed sai-lor hang-ing down be-hind, Whip jam-bo-ree, whip jam-bo-ree, O Jen-ny get your oat-cakes done.

Syncopation occurs at four places in this song — each time before the word 'jamboree'.

Practise these melodies with voice and instrument. Listen carefully to another pair's performance. Check that their syncopated rhythm is accurate. Suggest ways of improving their performance.

More syncopation p.99

A Welcome Song

For those who have been away –
and for new arrivals –
a welcome song is just the thing!

Wel - come, wel - come, we're pleased to know you!

Wel - come, wel - come, there's much to show you!

Now you are here we shall have ce - le - bra - tion,

All of the neigh - bours have an in - vi - ta - tion.

Here is a syncopated verse.
Perform it and practise it.
Compose a welcome song based on this rhythm.
You may use the words provided,
or make up new ones.

Composing with syncopation (1)　　p.101

Caribbean rhythm

1. Goin' to the market, take a rickety ride,
Goin' to the market, take a rickety ride,
Buy some coconuts, take me home again,
Buy some coconuts, take me back home.

2. Goin' to the market, take a rickety ride,
Goin' to the market, take a rickety ride,
Buy little 'tatoes, take me home again,
Buy little 'tatoes, take me back home.

3. Goin' to the market, take a rickety ride,
Goin' to the market, take a rickety ride,
Buy bananas, then you take me home again,
Buy bananas, then you take me back home.

First

Tap a pulse (in 4/4 time), and speak the words to a rhythm which includes syncopation.
Notice how the 3rd and 4th lines need a different rhythm in each verse.
Write down the rhythm for each verse (these 4/4 rhythms might help):

Compare your rhythms with the work of a partner.

Then

- Write a melody to your rhythm, using staff notation;
- use a doh hexachord on G (key signature = F sharp), with a change to lah tonality at a suitable place;
- give your melody a West Indies style, to match the words;
- sing your melody and play it on suitable instruments. (Use steel pans, if you have them.)

32 Composing with syncopation (2)   p.102

A Czechoslovakian melody

This melody from Czechoslovakia changes tonality.

2 bars lah hexachord	2 bars lah hexachord	2 bars doh pentachord	2 bars lah hexachord

With a partner, sing this melody to solfa; then sing it to the words.
Perform the song as a class choir.

Good night, be-lo-ved, good night, good night; God keep you safe in his watch-ful sight.

Good night, dear, mo-ther's here; Sweet be the dreams of your sleep to-night.

The Natural Minor scale on E p.103

33

A Ukrainian melody

Play this melody on a keyboard or on pitched percussion.
Perform the piece as a class orchestra,
using all available instruments.

This melody from Ukraine uses the Natural Minor scale.
Within the scale, it changes tonality.
The tone-set is: l-s-f-m-r-d-t₁-l₁.
It has a range of one octave.

The Natural Minor scale on D   p.105

A Russian melody

This is a Russian folk melody.
Sing the melody several times with a partner.
Each time you sing, use one of the blocks below to fill the missing section.

Which do you like best?
Can you guess which one belongs to the original melody?

Rewrite the last four bars to produce a different ending for the melody.
Remember that you will need to end on D (lah).

Working with the Natural Minor scale p.105   35

Styles in music

This course has used melodies in different styles from many countries and regions of the world, including England, Wales, Scotland, France, Germany, Sweden, Hungary, Czechoslovakia, Serbia, Ukraine, Russia, Israel, and the Caribbean.

Style in music is influenced by many things, including history, custom, climate and neighbours.

The melody on this page is from Greece.
Sing the melody to solfa and look closely at its features.
Copy the box on page 37.
Then analyse the melody by the headings in the box.

Styles with the Natural Minor scale (1)   p.106

Greek / English melody compared

The song on this page is from England. This melody, and the Greek melody on page 36, are natural minor melodies. But they are quite different in style.

There were three gyp-sies a-come to my door, And down-stairs ran this a-la-dy O! The one sung high and a-no-ther sung low, And a-no-ther sung Bon-ny, Bon-ny Bis-cay O!

Sing this melody and analyse it in your copy of the box.

Compare your analysis of the two songs.

Which features are the same?
Which features are different?

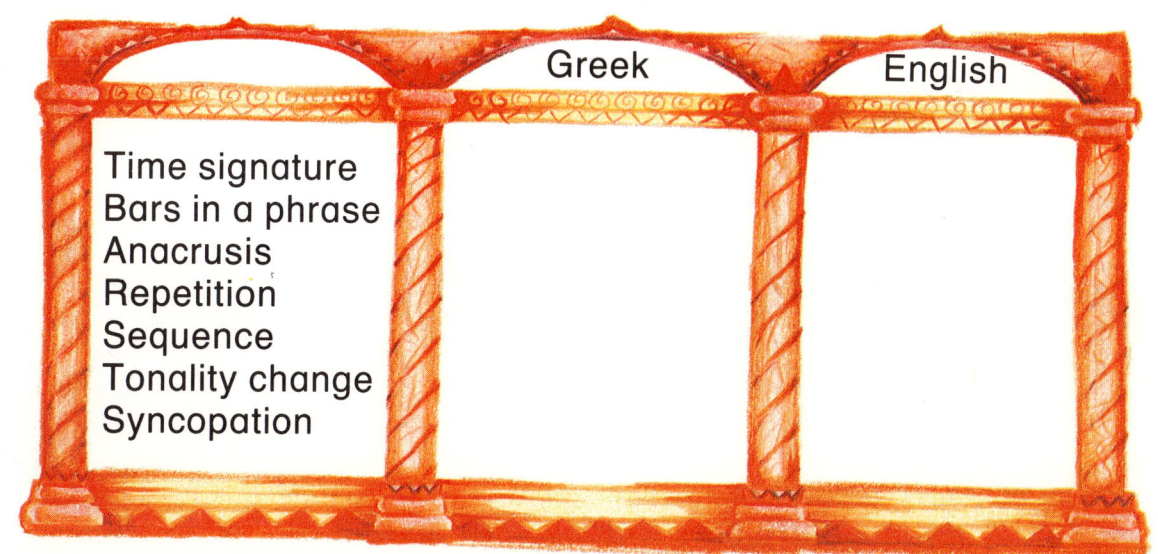

	Greek	English
Time signature		
Bars in a phrase		
Anacrusis		
Repetition		
Sequence		
Tonality change		
Syncopation		

Styles with the Natural Minor scale (2) p.106

A Portuguese melody

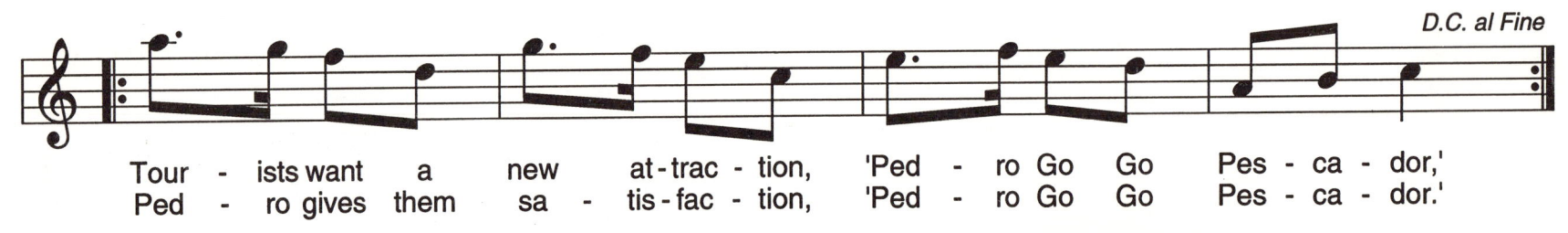

lah

Ne - ver a - gain will sun - lit wa - ters, Bright with dawn, see Ped - ro fish - ing,
Beached is the boat that took him sai - ling, Blue white bays of Por - tu - gal.

Tour - ists want a new at - trac - tion, 'Ped - ro Go Go Pes - ca - dor,'
Ped - ro gives them sa - tis - fac - tion, 'Ped - ro Go Go Pes - ca - dor.'

D.C. al Fine

With a partner, perform this melody on an instrument, with all repeats.
Then sing it with the words.

This is the structure of the melody:

Section	A	B	A
Phrase	A Av*	B B	A Av

*'Av' means 'A variant' – a phrase which differs only slightly from phrase A.

The Natural Minor on A (1)   p.107

The Natural Minor

Now make the melody on page 38 longer by adding a new section (section C).

Use this extended structure.
Notice that section C will be based on doh, rather than lah.

Section	A		B		A		C		A	
Phrase	A	Av	B	B	A	Av	C	C	A	Av
Tonality	Minor		Minor		Minor		Major		Minor	

Write a different version of your new, extended melody by changing the time signature to $\frac{6}{8}$.
Keep your rhythms simple.
Write in staff notation.

The Natural Minor on A (2)   p.107

The Authentic Major

With a partner, compare these two scales.

See the ⌒ sign where the semitones occur.

Extending the lah hexachord by one note (s) makes the *Natural Minor scale.*

$l - t - \widehat{d - r} - m - \widehat{f - ⓢ} - l$

Extending the doh hexachord by one note (t) makes the *Authentic Major scale.*

$d - r - \widehat{m - f} - s - l - \widehat{ⓣ - d}$

Sing the Authentic Major scale to these rhythms.

Each time, choose a starting note at a different position on the scale.

Sing scales which start by descending.
Sing scales which start by ascending.

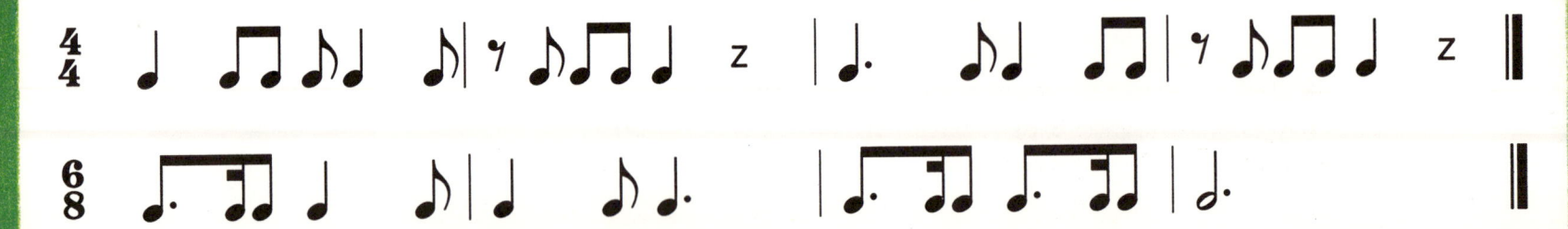

Working with melodies

With a partner, sing these two authentic major melodies.
Both start with d¹ and then descend in pitch.
Notice where the semitones occur.

¾ | d' d' d' | t t t | l t d' | s. | f f f | m m m | r m r | d. | d r m | d r m | d r m | f |
| r m f | r m f | r m f | s. | d' t l | s f m | r d r | d. ||

doh
4/4
U - pon Paul's stee - ple stands a tree, As full of ap - ples as can be, The lit - tle boys of Lon - don Town, They run with hooks to pull them down, And then they run from hedge to hedge, Un - til they come to Lon - don Bridge.

Write the top melody in staff notation (doh = C), changing the starting note to the fourth phrase so that it provides a different sequence to follow the third phrase.
Rewrite the lower melody so that it has as many passing notes as possible.
Perform your revised melodies.

The Authentic Major (2) p.108

'Tingalayo'

'Tingalayo' is a West Indian song using the Authentic Major (doh = C).

Sing it with a partner, looking for syncopation and sequence.

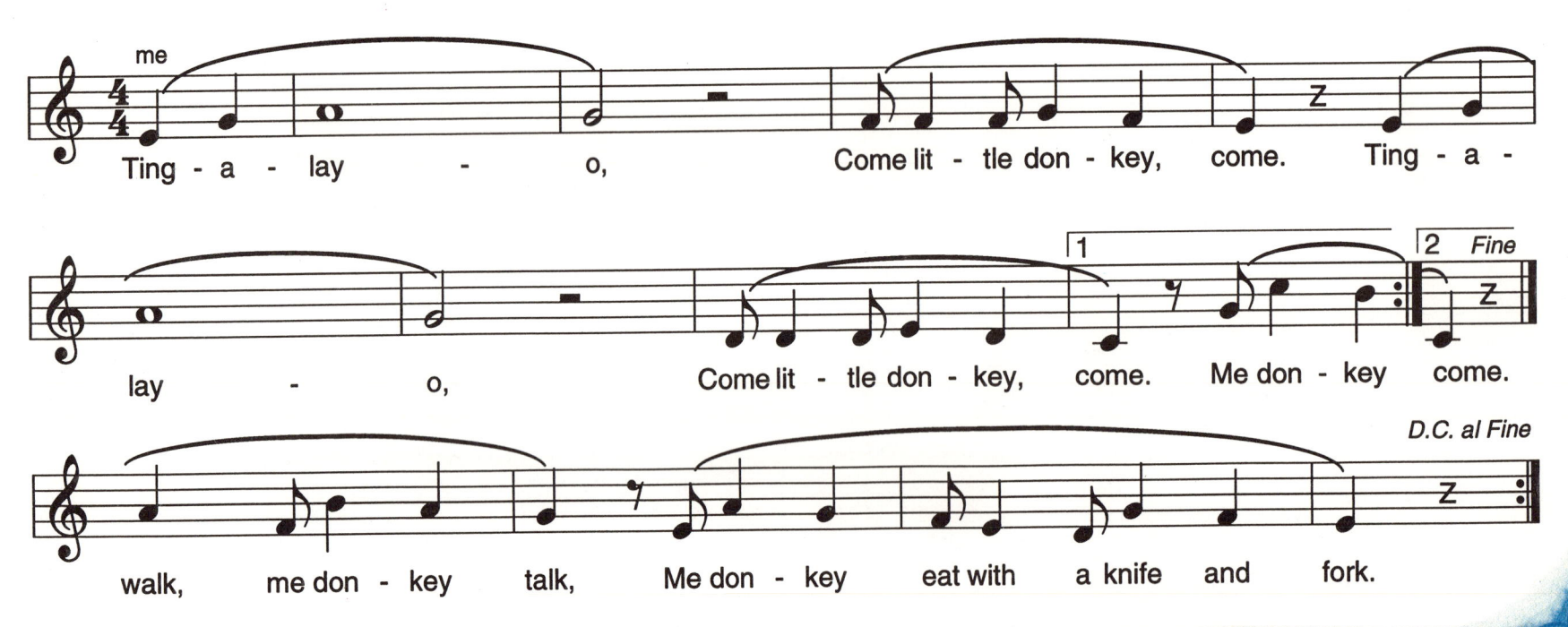

[Musical score with lyrics:]
Ting-a-lay - o, Come lit-tle don-key, come. Ting-a-lay - o, Come lit-tle don-key, come. Me don-key come. Me don-key walk, me don-key talk, Me don-key eat with a knife and fork.

D.C. al Fine

One partner taps this 4-bar ostinato, while the other sings the song, or plays the melody on an instrument.

42 Working with the Authentic Major (1)   p.109

A donkey song

Work with a partner.

Compose a melody (Authentic Major) with syncopation, using these words:

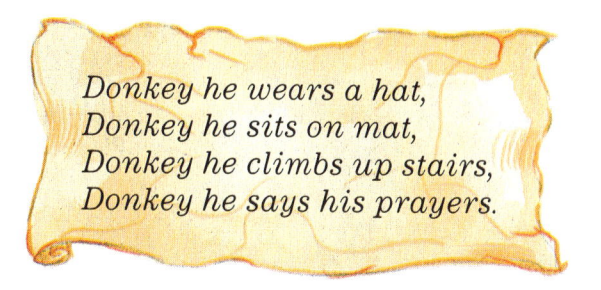

Donkey he wears a hat,
Donkey he sits on mat,
Donkey he climbs up stairs,
Donkey he says his prayers.

Write your melody in staff notation, based on one of these scales:

Authentic Major scales:

doh   doh   doh

Now devise a rhythm accompaniment for your melody, using two kinds of percussion instrument.

Compose two rhythms or two rhythm ostinati, and write them down.

Rehearse and perform your song.

Working with the Authentic Major (2)   p.109

Musical clocks

Every hour, as the minute-hand reaches number 12, this delicate mantelpiece clock plays a melody lasting 20 seconds. The melody sounds rather like a musical box.

The manufacturers have asked you to compose a suitable melody for their new range of clocks.

Arrange your completed melody for performance by this small group of instruments:
glockenspiel
xylophone
small wood block
+ one other instrument of your choice.

Rehearse and perform your clock music.

Refer to the analysis box below and decide whether you wish to make any alterations or additions.

Analysis

Number of bars	10
Phrase structure	A B A C Av
Bars per phrase	2.2.2.2.2.
Staff notation	doh = F
Rhythm-solfa	
Time signature	2/4
Rhythm-set	
Tone-set	d'-t-l-s-f-m-r-d
Other features	Sequence

44 Musical clocks   p.110

Major scales in two parts

The upper part uses all the notes of the Authentic Major.
The lower part uses all the notes of the Plagal Major.
With a partner learn both parts.
Then sing the piece together, in two parts.

Write the music in staff notation (doh = F).
Play this two-part arrangement from memory, using two melodic instruments.

The Plagal Major (1) p.111 45

With (or without) . . .

This melody was composed for the Walt Disney film *Pinocchio*.

I've got no strings to hold me down, To make me fret or make me frown,
I've got no strings so I have fun, I'm not tied up to a - ny - one,
I had strings but now I'm free, There are no strings on me.
How I love my li - ber - ty, There are no strings on me.

Fine

Hi - o the mer - ri - o, I'm as hap - py as can be.

D.C. al Fine

I want the world to know No - thing e - ver wor - ries me.

The shape of this melody is *angular* – rather like the awkward movement of a puppet.
Use an analysis sheet to analyse this melody. Analyse Reading Sheet 19A in the same way.

Working with a partner, invent musical phrases which have angular shape.

46 Puppet project (1)   p.112   19A

... strings attached

Compose the theme tune for a puppet show.

Choose from the following:
- A puppet dance, performed by suitable instruments.
- A song performed by the main puppet character.

(Devise your own words, according to the story you have in mind; e.g. a happy song in which the puppet sings about the advantages of being able to move compared with a mere doll.)

Working as a class, you might write a complete puppet show of your own. Perhaps you could make your own puppets and stage, and agree upon a storyline before composing the music.

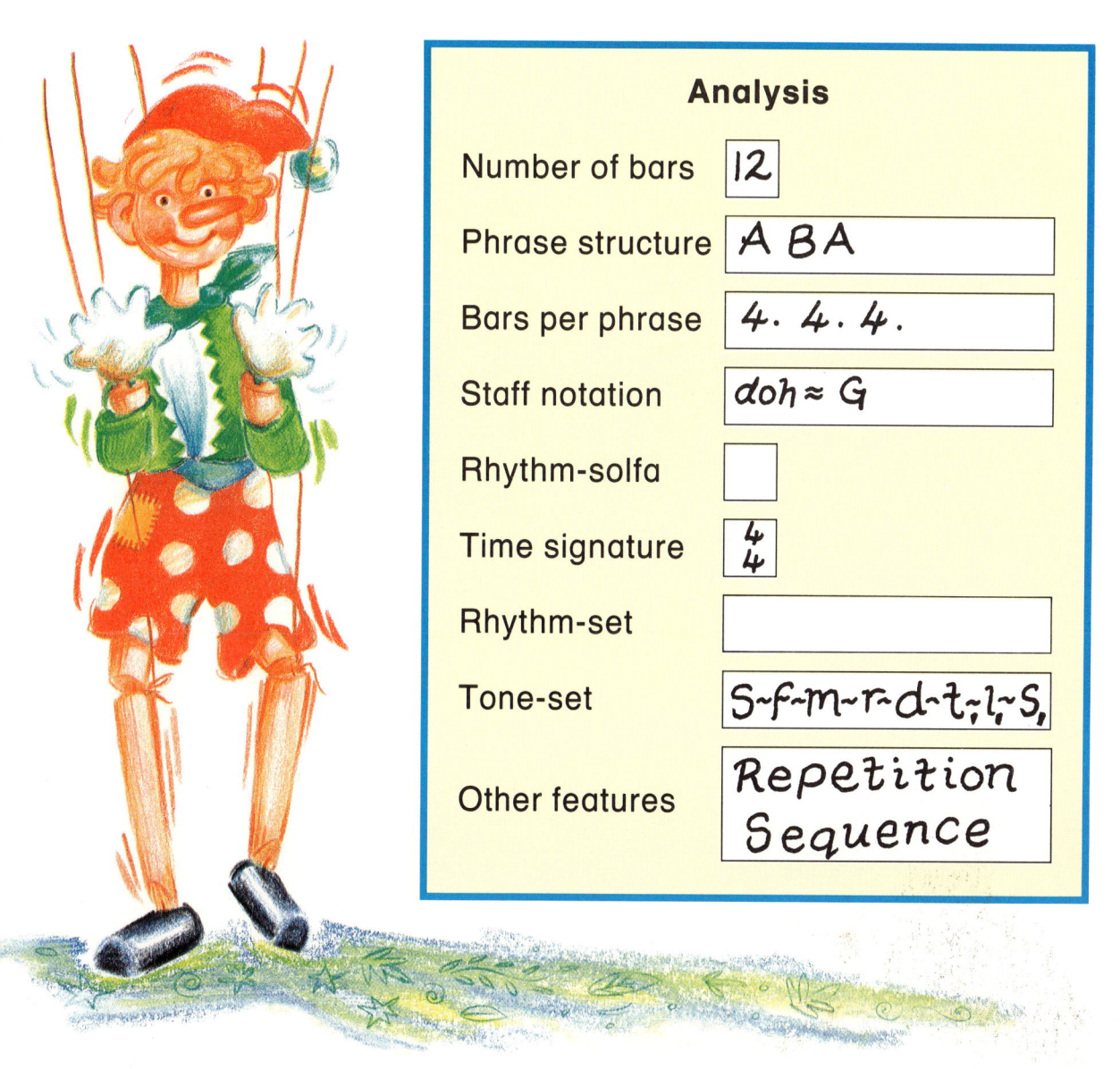

Analysis

Number of bars	12
Phrase structure	A B A
Bars per phrase	4. 4. 4.
Staff notation	doh ≈ G
Rhythm-solfa	
Time signature	4/4
Rhythm-set	
Tone-set	s-f-m-r-d-t,-l,-s,
Other features	Repetition Sequence

Puppet project (2) p.112

Dance to your daddy

This melody uses the Plagal Major on G.
It is a folk melody from Northumberland in the north of England.

Play it on an instrument.
Learn it by heart, and then teach yourself to play it from memory in the keys of F and C.

Ask your teacher how you could add a drone to this melody.

48 The Plagal Major (2) p.113